A CONNOISSEUR'S GUIDE TO ANTIQUE

GLASS

A CONNOISSEUR'S GUIDE TO ANTIQUE GLASS

RONALD PEARSALL

TODTRI

This book was designed and produced by TODTRI Book Publishers
P.O. Box 572, New York, NY 10116-0572
Fax: (212) 695-6984
e-mail: todtri@mindspring.com

Printed and bound in Singapore

ISBN 1-57717-153-5

Visit us on the web!
www.todtri.com

Author: Ronald Pearsall

Publisher: Robert M. Tod
Editor: Nicolas Wright
Art Directorr: Ron Pickless
Typesetting & DTP: Blanc Verso UK

CONTENTS

INTRODUCTION

It is easy to understand the manufacture of most antiques. Anyone can make pottery by shaping a piece of ordinary clay and putting it in a household oven. It is not so easy to make glass because of the high temperatures required and it needs more skill to carry out the process. But it is made from the cheapest and simplest of materials – sand, quartz or flint with a flux to fuse it together. The flux can be obtained from wood ash, or seaweed ash, as well as lead oxide, and although lead oxide was used in ancient times the possibilities were not fully recognized until the 1670s, when it revolutionised the making of drinking glasses, the prime achievement in British glass.

Once fused, glass is somewhat confusingly known as "metal", and it becomes the most versatile of materials. It can be blown, moulded, cast, or carved, it can be made in several layers so that sections can be cut out to reveal the layer below (cameo glass), and it can be engraved, enamelled, gilded, or painted, or "flashed" where an article of plain glass is dipped in molten coloured glass and the surface then has parts removed to make a pattern. These removed segments, often geometric, leave "sharp" edges, like cut glass, an effect that cannot be achieved by moulding.

The most common method used for making narrow-necked containers is creating a core of sand or mud, dipping in liquid glass, smoothing the surfaces, and then removing the core. Handles and feet are added as required, applied by a rod with a blob of molten glass on the end. Molten glass cools very slowly and is malleable for about three-quarters of an hour. Much can be done with decoration and additions in that period.

While molten, glass can be drawn out into long filaments ("spun glass"), which can be wrapped around the main body of the piece, form connections between protrusions on the article, or, in popular art, emulate spars and rigging in that traditional seaside-resort souvenir, the spun-glass ship, often made on the spot for the tourists.

Above: A Roman glass mosaic bowl from about 100 BC.

Opposite: The most famous piece of glass in the world, the Roman Portland Vase. In 1845 it was smashed by a lunatic in the British Museum, repaired, and endlessly copied by Wedgwood and other manufacturers.

EARLY GLASS

The most important event in the history of glass was in the first century BC when it was discovered that molten glass could be blown into a bubble using a pipe. This bubble could be shaped into the most intricate of shapes, either into a pre-formed mould or into a sphere, which could then be drawn out to form any kind of shape. The discovery was made in Syria, but there are many theories as to when and where glass was first used. The most conventional is that the ancient Egyptians discovered it by accident when they were making pottery, another that Phoenician merchants found that beneath their cooking pot was a curious unknown substance, formed from the mixing of sand with the ashes of their fire. However, there is no doubt that the Near and Middle East was where glass was first made, probably in Mesopotamia (Iraq) or northern Syria. Glass vessels have been found in these countries dating back to about 1500 BC.

The Egyptians thought glass would make a good substitute for pottery and used it in beads, and although they made crude bottles with a zigzag decoration derived from their pottery ornamentation, their first major achievement came with mosaic glass. Glass rods were built up into bundles, with a cross-section like seaside rock, fused into sheets, reheated, and then put into clay moulds to produce open vessels. The patterns on these colourful vessels could be simple and geometric, or complicated, and sometimes tiny particles of gold were put into the mix.

Glass is coloured by variations in the mix. Sometimes it is wanted, when substances such as oxides of copper or iron were introduced, sometimes it is not. One of the aims of the early glass-makers was to get pure transparency, which was not easy, as something had to be added to counter the natural glass colour. Soda glass from seaweed had a yellowish or greenish tinge, and it was only with Venetian glass and the addition of manganese to the molten metal that something approaching perfect translucency was achieved. Even then the glass was faintly tinged, though in a pleasant way which made the glass warmer. The Venetians called this glass *cristello*, and we know it as crystal, though it has altered its meaning and is now a general-purpose term for good-quality hand-made glass. It was named *cristello*

Above: A German characteristic glass beaker with sea-creature decoration from 300 AD.

Opposite: A display of early glass, from primitive times up to the tenth century AD, including glass from Mesopotamia, Rome, Egypt, and elsewhere in the Middle East.

Overleaf: Examples of early pre-Roman core-formed glass, probably fourth or third century BC. Functional vessels are difficult to attribute, as glass makers moved from country to country.

Above: An unusual Egyptian opaque red glass amulet of a Tyet girdle or Isis knot from 1150 – 1070 BC.

Opposite: A scent bottle in the form of a head from Syria, probably 100 – 200 AD. Though dating glass is always approximate as it ages in a totally different way to any other substance. Although subject to "glass sickness" it does not spontaneously disintegrate.

because it was like the valuable natural substance rock crystal.

Engraving on glass was known in Egypt from the fifteenth century BC, and in the succeeding centuries it became increasingly sophisticated. Enamel painting was exploited, as was cameo glass, layered glass usually white on dark blue, though the triumph of this art form was to come in Rome in the first century AD with the Portland Vase in the British Museum, smashed by a vandal, repaired, and imitated in his inimitable blue-and-white pottery by Wedgwood, still made, still popular, one of the great antique icons.

With the ascendancy of Rome, migratory Syrians and Egyptians helped to establish a Roman glass industry. The Italians soon outshone their teachers, producing novel vessels of a network design, the *diatreta*, of amazing virtuosity, held together by fragile struts, as well as glass mirrors, backed by tin or lead, which replaced polished metal. Fine spectacular glass continued to be made in the Near East and later to other Islamic countries such as Persia, which exported to India and where an industry sprung up.

Ordinary utilitarian glass spread through the Roman Empire, and each conquered nation contributed its own characteristic, though

when the empire began to collapse glass-making shifted to Gaul and then to Germany, where Cologne was the centre of the industry. A speciality of Cologne was the *Schlangenfadengläser*, "snake thread" glasses, in which beakers and goblets were adorned with fantastic trailing ribbons of coloured glass. Little pockets of glass-making appeared throughout Europe, but they were not significant.

However, this was only a brief interlude. With the collapse of western civilization, glass centres ceased to exist and glass-making became a home industry, isolated glass-houses pitched in forests which gave them the fuel, with an itinerant work force which moved from place to place. It was a prosaic industry, producing nothing of consequence, though glass-making prospered in the Near and Middle East until the fourteenth century, with Syria and Egypt joined by Mesopotamia (Iraq) as the major glass producers. They made glass that was the wonder of the west and highly treasured by the rich and powerful, mounted as reliquaries, invaluable heirlooms, even though the objects themselves, such as mosque lamps, were alien to the western world. Although most of the permutations of glass had been run through, the Egyptians produced a curious "lustre" glass, but no complete example survives.

An interesting parallel can be found in pottery. While European ceramics

Right: A small antique Egyptian glass bottle for medicinal or perfumery use. The Egyptians took glass out of the purely functional field and made it fine art. A good deal of Egyptian glass remains thanks to archaeologists.

were going through a dull unprofitable period, Persian tin-glazed pottery of great beauty was finding its way into Spain (the Hispano-Moresque pottery) and thence throughout Europe, eventually being called *faience*, or Delft, which was the most stylish ceramic form made in Europe before the introduction of porcelain.

When war split the Near and Middle Eastern states, the pendulum swung towards Europe, and Venice in particular, through its strong trading links with the east, though the Venetian industry had started up independently without an inflow of émigrés. Venetian glass of the fifteenth century and later is certainly one of the most diverse and adventurous, owing little to the glass of the past and introducing new features such as the "air twist" (trapping bubbles of air in stems of glasses and other containers) and exploring an amazing range of new

Above: A selection of Roman glass: a two-handled amber flask, a translucent light brown flask, a glass bowl, and a green two-handled flask. It would be more than 1,000 years before the secret of clear glass was discovered by the Venetians.

Above: A high-quality dark-amber mould-blown vase from the Eastern Mediterranean from about the fifth century AD. There are two types of blown glass; "free" blown into the air, and blown into a shaped mould.

rich colours. Designs were influenced by metalwork, especially silver, by contemporary painting, and by the discovery of the applied arts of the ancient civilizations.

Venice produced an enormous quantity of beads, both for wear and for trading purposes with the less civilised nations, and their coloured glass was breath-taking in its vivacity and beauty, but it was the colourless glass that was valued most. *Cristello* could be worked very thin, and although the first objects were simple, later ones became enormously complex. Plain glass was inset with strands of white opaque glass to produce a magical effect. The Venetians also evolved a crackle effect, by dipping plain hot glass into cold water, or by rolling glass vessels over a bed of glass splinters ("ice glass"). They also made glass that imitated gemstones.

Glass-makers were working in Venice as early as 982, a guild was formed in 1255, and in 1291 glass-houses on a large scale were established on the island of Murano just off the coast at Venice. They were sited there because of the fear of fire in Venice itself. Glass-workers were virtually imprisoned on the island of Murano and forbidden to have contact with the outside world. The Doge intended to keep his secrets. Some workers who escaped were assassinated. But as with porcelain, there is no technological advance that will stay a secret, and what was unique to Venice would soon be known to the outside world. Some workers did get away and set up on their own. Their products are known as *facons de Venise* (style of Venice) and it is impossible to determine their country of origin. Many of these glass workers settled in the Low Countries, but very few found their way to Britain.

By the beginning of the sixteenth century, rich blues, purples and greens of an intensity previous only dreamed of were much used. But the most popular was opaque white and it was during this period that Venice managed to produce the first porcelain, long before Meissen It was a short-lived project as it was expensive, fragile, and unreliable. If there was a fault in Venetian glass it was that it, too, was fragile, and could not be engraved with anything but a diamond point, and frequently this was not possible either. However, there was sufficient variety in the enamelling and the bravura of the set pieces. Not all the Venetian glass-makers were involved in bold forays into the future; there were four classes of workers – who made rosaries, window glass, beads (the lowest in the craft) as well as display pieces. It was an early example of commercial specialisation in the applied arts. The higher echelons of glass-makers enjoyed great prestige, and sometimes married into the nobility.

There was a huge demand throughout Europe for Venetian glass, especially the more dramatic pieces, and this possibly stemmed innovation in other countries.

Amongst the most unusual of the Venetian products were the drinking glasses. Accustomed as we are in the western world to slim stems of a refined design, the Venetian glasses had

Below: A blue cameo vase recovered from Pompeii, buried under volcanic ash from the eruption of Mount Vesuvius in AD 79 until the town's discovery in 1748.

stems in the forms of extravagant dragons, and other creatures, more than twice the height of the actual bowl. Their all-over enamelled designs of flowers and fruit on vases and containers make it difficult to believe that these are in fact glass. It is traditional to find Venetian glass unsurpassable, but the very exuberance becomes overcharged and the delight in expertise is often tiring, too much crammed into a small area, as in the tazzas (display bowls) where enamelling and gilding are both profusely employed. Jugs in the shape of ships may have been clever and amusing but they were hardly useful.

The decline of Venetian glass was as dramatic as its rise. By the beginning of the seventeenth century glass-houses in the Venetian style had been established in Bologna, Genoa, and Ferrara, which also had access to Venice's secret ingredients – powdered marble and crushed white pebbles from the River Po . The Draconian regime of the Doge declined when influential members of the guild had enough power in their own right to move elsewhere in Italy. This co-incided with the decline of Venice itself (it must be remembered that Venice was a major naval power). From the middle of the seventeenth century Venetian glass was in free fall.

Before the influence of Venetian glass reached the outside world, British and European glass is not impressive, cloudy, inclined to be brittle, and used for utilitarian purposes. With the exception of stained glass. Just as the Church was responsible for great architecture in the form of churches and cathedrals, so too was it involved in almost every form of artistic endeavour.

It is important to realise that in the eleventh century, when stained glass was first being used for figurative work rather than simple

Above: The Roman "Lycurgus" cup of the fourth century AD. It was customary to give important pieces fanciful names.

Opposite: A third-century vase with a snake-thread ornament from Cologne.

abstract shapes, there was a high level of expertise, though this found its expression in artefacts which have not come down to us, such as costume, or in articles which were essential for survival and which reflected social and national struggle, such as weaponry and armour. Art for art's sake would have been as incomprehensible then as it is today. The monks of the time probably did not realise they were creating objects of beauty when they were writing and painting their illuminated manuscripts; these, like stained glass, were to the glory of God and the practitioners merely supplicants.

Stained glass reached its peak in France and Britain in the twelfth and thirteenth century with the cathedrals of Chartres, Saint Denis, Le Mans, Bourges, Chalons-sur-Marne, Saint-Chapelle in France and York Minster and Canterbury in England. Crown glass was used. Crown glass is best known for the "bull's-eye" windows in old houses. It is made by spreading a blown bubble onto a flat sheet by rapid motion of the rod. The details in stained glass were painted on in black enamel, and the various pieces of glass were held in place in a framework of lead. Designs were derived from illuminated manuscripts. Improvements in glass technology in the fourteenth century made larger pieces of glass available, and in the sixteenth century transparent enamel pigments meant that it was possible to paint directly onto large pieces of glass without having to build a window together like a jigsaw puzzle. By this time there was less interest, though there was a great revival in the nineteenth century when stained glass was used on a monumental scale for churches, private houses, and public buildings such as town halls. And it was a trend that continued throughout the twentieth century, and mercifully many houses of the 1920s and 1930s retain their stained glass door panes and windows, many of great charm and individuality. Early domestic stained glass, first seen in France in the fourteenth century, portrayed

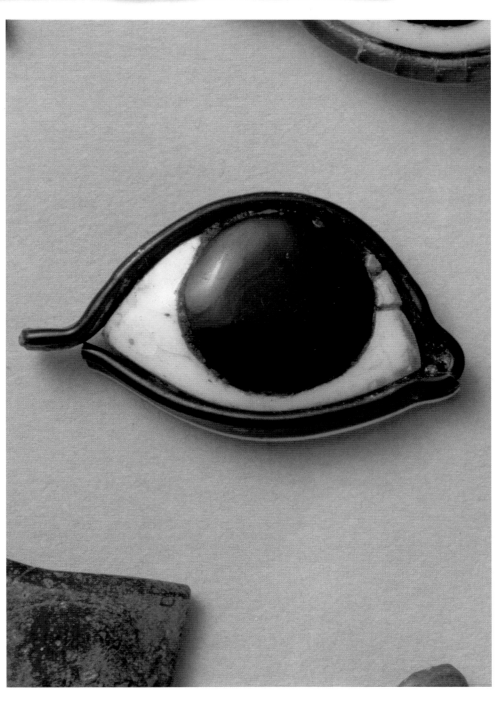

Above: A sample of the exquisite craftsmanship displayed by glass makers in the centuries before Christ, a sequence of inlays including a glass inlay of an eye.

Opposite: A dark brown glass vessel of Eastern Mediterranean origin, maybe fifth or sixth century AD. Brown was one of the easiest colours to get; it was, with green, the "natural" colour to get using the everyday ingredients of glass.

Left: A selection of early vases: a blown marbled flask, an amphoriskos, a translucent green flask, and an "acorn" amphoriskos, from the first century AD and Eastern Mediterranean in origin.

allegories, mythological scenes, and especially coats-of-arms.

In the nineteenth century many great artists were involved in stained glass, such as William Morris in Britain, and J. L. C. Tiffany and J. La Farge in the United States. In 1827 Sèvres opened a studio dedicated to stained glass.

Early bottles were of salt-glazed stoneware, and the first glass bottles arrived in the seventeenth century. One of the key drinking vessels, still popular in Germany, was the *Roemer*, in the shape of a sphere with the top sliced off on a flat base. British glass was of little consequence, astonishing considering the superb stained glass of earlier times, and although glass was first made in America in 1608 in Jamestown, Virginia, a year after settlers arrived, it took its tone from England, and produced only crude drinking vessels, beads, bottles and crown or window glass. From some time after 1650 glass-making moved to New Amsterdam (afterwards New York), where there were two glass-houses, but although the influence was Dutch the products were still crude, though the Dutch themselves were adept at engraved glass.

Other substances, such as pewter, were used for drinking vessels, as they

Above: A Persian or Islamic dark green glass stem cup of the fifth to the seventh century.

Opposite: British glass was almost non-existent until the amazing flowering of stained glass in the Middle Ages.

still are in a few old-fashioned country public houses in Britain. It was only when there was an underlying demand for superior drinking glasses by connoisseurs of wine and liqueurs that there was an improvement. And the British glass-makers had invented a new kind of glass which was to change the whole nature of colourless glass, and was to mark Britain's greatest achievement in glass – the drinking glass.

BOTTLES & FLASKS

The first noteworthy bottles were made of salt-glazed stoneware, not glass, and they are globular vessels bearing a grotesque mask known as Bellarmines after Cardinal Bellarmine (1542 – 1621) though the bottles themselves certainly predated him. There is a Bellarmine in the Tower of London dated 1562 when the cardinal was only eighteen and not the drunken roué depicted on the bottle. They were popular until the nineteenth century, first produced in England by John Dwight at the Fulham Pottery in London in the late seventeenth century.

The British glass bottle industry began in the early seventeenth century, and the bulk of its output was wine bottles. In 1696 there were 90 glasshouses in England and Wales, most of them in London and Bristol and 42 of these produced bottles. From 1623 to 1860 it was illegal to sell wine by the bottle, and because of heavy taxation on glass (which also had a great effect on the drinking glass) bottles were expensive to buy. Wine was ordered by the barrel from the merchants, and transferred by the merchant to the owners' bottles, and for ease of identification the bottles had a glass seal or disc applied to them on the side which was embossed with the owner's name, initials or crest and often a date.

The earliest known seal (without a bottle) dates from 1652, the oldest seal with bottle 1657, bearing a head believed by some to be Charles I as he has always been a picaresque figure (though the legend is unlikely as he died on the scaffold in 1649). Dating was not neces-

Above: A Roman perfume bottle of the second or third century AD.

Opposite: A silver-mounted diamond-engraved serving bottle 1685 – 1690 attributed to Willem Mooleyser. During the great age of English drinking-glass manufacture, plain glasses were sent to Holland for engraving and then returned.

Above: A Roman cosmetic bottle accompanied by a spatula of the first/second century AD. A surprising number of Roman perfume bottles exist, perhaps because they were small and compact and not so susceptible to damage as larger glass containers.

sarily a fad when the stoppers were made of cork; a little-known worm eats cork at a very slow rate, and after 35 years corks need to be replaced. The law about bottles was widely flouted by inn keepers who sold wine in bottles without seals.

From 1620 – 1660 bottles are so rare as to be prized museum purposes, but the shape persisted. Known as "shaft and globe" they had a roundish bulbous body and a very long neck, with a rim near the top so that the stopper could be tied down. The neck became shorter, the body more onion-shaped, and towards the beginning of the eighteenth century there was a tendency towards a mallet shape. From about 1730 bottles were made using moulds. These were more cylindrical and slightly taller while around 1750 wine was being laid down in bins for maturing and the familiar wine bottle shape began to emerge.

The "seal" bottles were hand-made and consequently varied in shape, sometimes lop-sided, sometimes rather comical, and their colours were dark, usually dark green or black, which was convenient as any impurities were masked. Not that they were important; the widespread use of decanters from the 1700s onwards got rid of the dregs. Some of the early bottles seem to be made from paler glass, but this is largely due to long incarceration in the soil, and the glass has begun to decay. These have an oily look, and reflect rainbow colours, very decorative but not liked by dedicated collectors.

When bottles were hand-made they left a "pontil mark" on the base where the glass-maker finished his job. When the bottle was satisfactorily blown, the pipe was withdrawn and the surplus glass was removed with a pontil rod, leaving a scar. This could make the bottle

Above: A seventeenth-century wine bottle. About this time there 90 glass-houses in England and Wales, of which 42 produced bottles. The familiar wine-bottle shape was evolved about 1750.

unstable, so bottles were designed with a "kick-up" in the base, which, for tradition's sake, is still a feature of many wine bottles. When bottles were likely to fall over they were put in a wicker basket, rather like the Italian wine Chianti is presented today.

The reason for keeping wine horizontal in bins rather than vertically was part due to the Methuen Treaty between Portugal and England to undercut the French with favourable trade concessions. Portugal naturally produced port, and it became immensely popular, as did the apparent spread of gout, legendarily supposed to result from a large intake of port. Port matures in the bottle and not a cask, and if stored upright it takes on the flavour of vinegar. Sideways the cork is always kept moist and swollen to keep the air out. It became the established way of storing wine in gentlemen's wine cellars, and was far more accessible to butlers and the like as the racks could be labelled and a rare vintage was not stuck at the back (though until recently vintage wine was not necessarily favoured).

The corking of wines varied over the years, with oiled hemp, leather or beeswax proving unreliable. Flush-fit corks arrived towards the end of the seventeenth century along with the necessary invention of the corkscrew. The "string ring" (the rim applied to early bottles) was retained even though it served no purpose.

With the widespread use of moulds and relaxations on tax on glass, millions of bottles were produced for every known liquid. Steel moulds replaced wooden moulds, which meant that the bottles could be sharply embossed with the name of the firm providing the beer, the soft drink, or whatever novelty was being promoted such as coloured water which purported to cure everything. Mineral water became

popular about 1840 and the bottles were usually aqua (nearly clear, faintly tinged with green), though Jacob Schweppe in the late 1790s had introduced the first commercial medicinal soda water. As all but wine bottles were kept upright, Schweppe used a pointed bottle which had to be laid on its side to prevent air escaping through the cork. These are known as "Torpedo" or "Hamilton" bottles and few date from earlier than 1830.

Bottles were assuming different shapes. Even beer bottles could be short and squat. Beer bottles often carried elaborate embossed pictorial trademarks, though embossing was considered only slightly less vulgar than the transfer printed designs or paper labels which supplemented embossing in the late nineteenth century.

The cork was replaced, except for wine, by a variety of stoppers – the screw-top (1872), the metal crown top of about 1892, the ceramic top operated by a swing mechanism attached to the neck, and, the

most interesting and innovative of them all, the marble top associated with the name of Hiram Codd. Codd's patent of 1872 was designed to keep the fizz in aerated drinks. A glass marble was trapped just below the neck and forced upwards against a rubber ring by the gas in the liquid. By means of a cap-with-plunger supplied with the bottle, the marble could be displaced and trapped behind two lugs. The contents then flowed freely. It was a cumbersome way to do a simple job, and the result could have been foreseen except by an inventor; small boys smashed the bottles to get at the marbles which were then used in games. The patent was easily broken although, surprisingly, Codd bottles lasted until 1930 and are still being made in India. Codd 's bottles were sufficiently known to spawn the catchphrase "Codswallop" meaning rubbish.

Beer bottles were usually dark to hide impurities, but they were comparatively late on the scene as beer was more often sold from the

keg. Those who drank away from the taverns and public houses (a curious phrase for drinking places dating from as early as 1669), collected the beer in pottery or metal containers. Gin and whisky were sometimes sold in pottery bottles, as well as pocket-sized glass flasks of various shapes. By the end of the nineteenth century automated glass-factories (rather than glass-houses) were producing 50,000 bottles a day, all sizes, all types, some fancifully shaped, some so distinctive that they became linked with the product (such as Coca-Cola and Bovril).

Bottles are one of the favourite starter collections, and they have all the right qualities. They come in an endless variety and can be subdivided (seal bottles, ink bottles, poison bottles, even milk bottles). They are largely cheap and the supply is endless – a Victorian rubbish tip can yield more than 10,000 bottles, although only a small proportion will be of any value. Few bottles except for "shaft and globe" types are out of the price range of the ordinary collector. Each specialised collecting area usually has its own news letter and web site.

Above: A wine bottle from Trengoff, Cornwall, dated 1704. Dating was important as periodically the flush-fitting corks (a feature introduced in the late seventeenth-century) had periodically to be replaced to avoid contaminating the wine.

Opposite: A bottle with a consumer's mark and date, 1698, from Cotehele House. Until 1860 it was illegal to sell wine in a bottle, and the wine was decanted into the drinkers' own bottles. Because of excise duty on glass, bottles were expensive, as was glass in general.

Ink bottles have countless dedicated collectors. For such mundane objects the variety is very large, ranging from simple square or round containers with a short neck to models of tents, cottages, igloos, and umbrellas, some having ridges for pens and grooves for pen nibs. Embossed detail was usually provided with, on the cottages, roof tiles and window shapes. The dark colours are preferred, especially blue, brown, and green, and most types have a jagged lip known as a "burst-top", not for economy but to grip the cork. The vast quantity was the consequence of the replacement of the quill pen by the steel-nib pen in the nineteenth century, and many factories, especially in Birmingham, Warwickshire, made nothing but millions upon millions of pen nibs prior to the invention of the typewriter, which remained something of an oddity until towards the end of the

century. Nibs are sometimes confusingly known as pens, thus the term pen-holder. Most ink bottles are indifferently made because they were for the mass market – the new board schools and thousands of offices; the better-off had silver inkstands with containers for more elegant square and round ink bottles in finer glass.

Among the most inventive bottles are poison bottles. These are usually dark blue, clearly marked as poison with dire warnings, but in the dark it was easy to take a swig, so bottles were shaped to make them distinctive or were wired up to elaborate alarm systems. There were bottles in the shape of coffins, wedges, skulls, bones, and even submarines (pre-World War I popular fiction rated submarines as the ultimate menace – which they nearly were). Many had their necks at strange angles or were covered with sharp projections. The coffin bot-

Above: One of a set of four gold and gem-set scent bottles, the tops about 1740, the glass and neck mounts much later, probably the late nineteenth-century. It was not unusual for Victorians to pick-and-mix in various ages and styles, but not at all common with glass.

Opposite: Three flat-sided bottles of about 1750. Bottles were never uniform; and certain liquids had their own particular bottles, or even bottles made from pottery.

tle dates from 1871, the wired-up bottle 1874. It was an age of innovation. 1887 brought a stopper incorporating a bell. The bone-shaped bottle was the invention of Edward Cone of Newark, New Jersey, After the accidental death of a professor from poisoning the Pharmaceutical Society asked for all poison bottles to be in triangular form, but the request was disregarded for the sake of novelty.

Glass in certain colours was associated with a particular range of products. Sulphur-yellow was likely to be perfume, white milk or opal glass was suitable for cosmetics. Square bottles were associated with gin, and in fact still are. Stoneware bottles were sacred to ginger beer and also to a lesser extent, vinegar and cider Glass feeding bottles were introduced to the UK in 1830, but a novelty feeding bottle had been introduced in Holland in 1784 which had a spherical end which could be removed and a tiny sponge was inserted. Perhaps the most elegant bottles were for perfume, which could be fitted out with sprays. Many perfume bottles were tiny, hardly more than an inch long, and the close-fitting glass stopper proved the most suitable, and far more chic than a cork. These became minor art objects in the 1920s and 1930s.

American bottles were not dissimilar to British bottles, but although Britain had bottles for brand-name beef extracts such as Oxo, Bovril, Valentine's Meat Juice, Bi-Win, Borthwick's Bouillon, some of them of American origin, distinctive coffee and sauce bottles, a small rectangular bottles for lemonade and other crystals (some shaped like the Eiffel Tower), there is one bottle that is known throughout the world – Coca-Cola, invented in 1902, and sold in a variety of different

Above: Most interesting for its provenance, this 1764 bottle is from All Soul's College, Oxford, perhaps the only university college in the world without any students, thus giving the Fellows of the college ample time to drink.

Wine bottles with seals named and dated from 1723 to 1835, a late date for seal bottles.

Left: A group of delicate Roman blown and mould blown glass cosmetics flasks, preserved in near-perfect condition.

shaped bottles until 1915 when the present-day "hobbleskirt" version made its appearance.

As for the curios, there is no end to them. They were particularly suited to paper labelling and stencilling, but many came to the fore when only embossing was practised. Along with the numerous patent medicines, some of which carry on today, there was Dadam's Microbe Killer in a dark glass rectangular bottle with embossing of a skeleton hitting a man on the head with a club. One will never know whether Turlington's Balsam of Life delivered its promise, though Elliman's Horse Embrocation, in a thin bottle like a laboratory gadget, certainly did. It was never meant for horses, but it was cunning advertising.

Above: A German seventeenth-century amethyst flask with a screw stopper. There were many different ways of closing a bottle, the screw-top, especially when fitted with rubber rings, being the most efficient.

Opposite: A beautifully decorated scent bottle, blown, cut, enamelled and gilded, attributed to Bristol, c. 1770.

ENGLISH GLASS

For a country with such massive documentation of the past, the history of British glass is fitful, periods of great innovation followed by centuries of mystery. The creators of stained glass in the great cathedrals and churches of the Middle Ages are anonymous, and do not appear to have been associated with any advances in domestic and display glass. All the quality glass was imported, and what little good glass was made was produced by glass-workers from abroad. As early as 758 the Abbot of Wearmouth appealed to the bishop of Mainz to send him artisans to manufacture "windows and vessels of glass, because the English were ignorant and helpless".

There is no evidence of domestic glass being made in England between the Roman occupation and the thirteenth century. There are some deeds referring to an application for twenty acres in Sussex in about 1230 for a "vitrearius", and fragments of glass from around this time have been excavated. In 1447 there is mention of glass being made for a chapel in Warwick which was superior to "Dutch, Venice or Normandy glass", but this was an isolated instance. In the sixteenth century there was a fashion for using glass vessels of an ornamental character, and King Henry VIII had a large collection of this glass, chiefly of Venetian manufacture, and in 1550 eight Venetian glass-makers were employed in or near the Tower of London.

Various glass-houses spread throughout the country sited in or near forests for the fuel. However, in 1615 timber was prohibited for use in glass-making to save these forests, and coal was used instead. The import of foreign glass was prohibited, giving a boost to the English

Above: Wine glasses came in all shapes and styles, with a variety of stems, the baluster being one of the most popular.

Opposite: Prior to Ravenscroft, English glass was dull and undistinguished. He made English wine glasses the envy of the world.

glass industry. During the English Civil War these restrictions lapsed, and imports from the continent resumed, but a glass industry was well established and in 1673 the diarist John Evelyn mentioned a visit to a glass-house in Greenwich "where glass was blown of finer metal than that of Murano" (the island off Venice where Venetian glass was made).

Be that as it may, the restoration of the monarchy in 1660 after the Civil War was perhaps the most important event in the history of English taste. The austerities of Cromwell's Commonwealth were forgotten and there was a yearning for high living and sophistication, epitomised by Restoration comedy, the triumph of walnut over oak in furniture, new styles of silver, and the rapid growth of a consumer society which demanded the best. There was also a spirit abroad of scientific enquiry. English glass was in the doldrums. The London Company of Glass-Sellers invited George Ravenscroft (1618 – 81) to investigate possible new glass technology, and perhaps find a substitute for *barilla* (the ash of seaweed used as a flux) which needed to be imported.

In 1675 Ravenscroft discovered that lead introduced into the metal created glass which was solid, heavy, and less fragile than Venetian glass and was also of brilliant transparency. It was more sluggish to work, and the techniques of the Venetian glass-makers were overturned. The use of lead glass led to the great period of English glass-making and its predominant icon – the drinking glass. It had a plain foot, a bowl and a stem with different-shaped protuberances or "knops". The methods of construction varied; a two-piece glass is one in which the stem and bowl are formed from one piece of metal, with the foot formed from a separate piece. A three-

Below: Irish glass is known principally by the name of Waterford, and this trumpet-shaped goblet commemorating the triumph of William of Orange dates from about 1720.

piece glass has the bowl, stem, and foot constructed separately then welded together.

Throughout the eighteenth century, there were endless variations on the stem. Besides the permutations of the knops, air bubbles could be introduced into the stem, which could be twisted out making an intricate pattern of air-lines. Opaque white threads could be set in the stem in the Venetian style, to marvellous effect. As the middle of the century approached a lighter glass was favoured, especially as an Excise Act of 1745 levied a considerable duty on glass by weight. Drinking glasses began to be engraved, and between about 1762 and 1780 there was a vogue for enamelling on clear glass. Newcastle-on-Tyne in the north east of England was a centre of experimentation and excellence in this field as in many others in glass-making.

Bowls were sometimes coloured, and came in a variety of shapes and sizes, made for specific drinks. Wine glasses had a capacity of two or three ounces, ale glasses had a relatively long bowl and were often decorated with hops and barley, and similar glasses with apple decoration were used for cider. Shorter ale glasses are known as dwarf ales. Cordials were popular drinks in the eighteenth century and were similar in strength to present-day liqueurs, and cordial glasses had small bowls. Drams were designed for spirit drinking, and had short stems, while flute glasses were fashionable for ratafia, a cordial flavoured with almonds, and either peaches or cherries. Rummers had large capacity bowls and a rudimentary stem, while a curiosity is the toastmaster's glass, with a deceptively small capacity so that he would remain sober. Goblets were usually over eight inches tall. Goblets became a popular type of glass in Victorian times in all mediums.

Above: A unique goblet enamelled with the royal coat of arms and the Prince of Wales' feathers made by one of the greatest names in British glass making, William Beilby of Newcastle-upon-Tyne about 1762, and thought to celebrate the birth of the future King George IV in that same year.

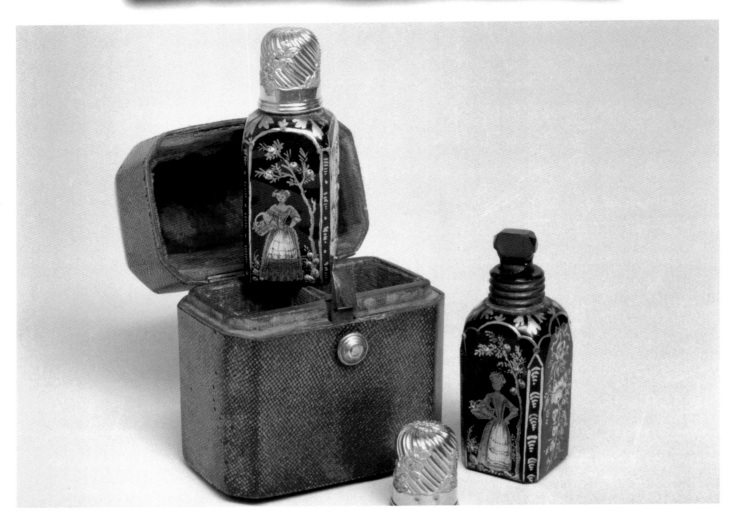

Above: A pair of blue scent bottles with gilt metal caps in a shagreen-covered case made about 1770. Many of these small bottles were of the highest quality and very expensive, and some had enamelled stoppers of exquisite delicacy.

Opposite: Wine glass with funnel bowl and a multiple spiral air twist stem, made by trapping air into the molten "metal" (the name for semi-liquid glass). It is engraved with the Jacobite (commemorating Charles Edward Stuart (Bonnie Prince Charlie) and his bid to gain the throne of England and Scotland in 1745) rose, with two buds. Such glasses are rare, and consequently much faked at a later date.

There were also glasses associated with sweetmeats which are sometimes called champagne glasses – though they would be difficult to drink from – and jelly glasses, which had a short stem and were often fitted with handles. There were seven basic bowl shapes – round funnel, trumpet, bell, bucket, ogee, ovoid, and conical. Engraving was done using a rotating copper wheel and an abrasive or by a diamond point. Stipple engraving needed great skill, and involved puncturing the surface of the glass with hundreds of dots. Plain glasses have often been engraved in recent times to increase the value. Especially prone to this are "Jacobite" glasses celebrating Bonnie Prince Charlie in exile after he failed to take over the British throne after the Stuart dynasty had been usurped by William III.

Not all eighteenth-century glass was lead glass; soda ash was still used as a flux. And not all the glasses are first rate. Nor were all the decanters, which were developed during the eighteenth century in tandem with glasses, were initially bottle-shaped but soon took on a distinctive character of their own. Decanter stoppers were ground individually for just those decanters – thus the problem when a decanter is lacking its stopper. From the 1770s coloured-glass decanters were made, often with gilded labelling, and some decanters are flat-bottomed, known as ships' decanters, and usually have sturdy rims on the neck so that they can be handled more safely by those in peril on

the sea or, more frequently, drunk. An interesting and superior off-
shoot from decanters was the claret jug, usually in a fretted metal
container, usually of silver.

To denote what the contents of bottles and decanters were silver
labels were hung by a chain around the neck. These are not only
interesting and often beautiful objects in themselves, but they demon-
strate the great range of liquors available to the British toper. They
date from the 1730s. During the Commonwealth period few drinks
other than ale and sack were drunk, but with the arrival of Charles II
tastes became more demanding and sophisticated.

Among the finest of eighteenth-century glass was Bristol blue. The
Bristol glass-houses were established in the 1740s, and although their
blue glass, often with gilded decoration, is best-known they also made
fine white glass, the equal of any in Europe. As with much glass, it is
impossible to establish where "Bristol blue" was made, because as
soon as a product became fashionable it was taken up elsewhere. The
Bristol manufacturers went out of production between 1780 and 1820
because the supplies of Silesian cobalt to colour the glass were cut off.

Britain had made the best drinking glasses in the world, and then
set out to make the best cut-glass. Lead glass with its innate brilliance
and diffractive qualities was especially suited to cutting, and dates
from about 1730. The main motifs were diamonds, crescents or trian-
gles, and the diamond honey-comb pattern was perhaps the most popular. Amongst the most important practitioners of this art was
Waterford in Ireland, started in 1784 with workers from Stourbridge

Left: A composite part table-service.
A selection of glasses, possibly Waterford in
Ireland from around 1830.

Right: An aesthetic movement stained glass and printed glass screen, the design attributed to J Moyr Smith.

Opposite: "Minstrel with cymbals". A Morris & Co. stained glass window drawn for the east window of St. John's church, Dalton, York, England.

in England, and closing in 1851 when the English competition became too overwhelming. Much glass was made in England and sent to Waterford to be cut. It is difficult to distinguish Waterford from other Irish glass factories in Cork and Dublin, and the slightly bluish tinge sometimes believed to be special to Waterford is found elsewhere.

Towards the close of the eighteenth century, in tune with the new Neo-Classical outlook, cut-glass became muted and more decorous, though diamonds, fluting, and parallel furrows continued to be used. Throughout the nineteenth century cut-glass was in overwhelming demand, and the deeper the cutting and the diversity of all-over patterning the better. In rooms lit by candles, oil lamps or gas the cut glass glittered and even tableware could take on the mantle of display pieces. Dismissed as "prickly monstrosities", Victorian cut-glass

*Above: The Breadalbane Amen glass.
Breadalbane is a remote district in Scotland
which gave its name to John Campbell, the
first Earl of Breadalbane (1635 – 1717).
He led an abortive Royalist uprising in 1654
against Oliver Cromell's Commonwealth.
He later became a staunch supporter of
William of Orange and ended his days as
an influencial member of government.*

brought out the worst in the buying public, and good glass-makers were going in a totally different direction.

Among the high-quality commercial glass was cranberry or ruby glass in red, much used in lamp shades especially in association with oil lamps, and in *épergnes*, centre pieces that incorporated candleholders, hanging baskets, vases and lustre drops. There was frequently a mirror base. One three-tier stand had 28 hanging baskets and towered six feet in height. The cranberry glass was often decorated with trailing strands of glass, and as the *épergne* was vulnerable the trumpet-shaped flower-holders were later made of metal. The first stands were registered in 1860, but those were in white, and cranberry proved to be the preferred colour. Cranberry was very popular in America, and more was produced there than in Britain. Another major producer, Bohemia, which was one of the pioneers, using gold in the mix to get the colour, though other methods were later discovered.

Thomas Webb and Sons of Stourbridge was established in 1837, making the customary range of domestic and display pieces, exhibiting at the Great Exhibition of 1851, and seemingly hardly different from other commercial glass-makers, though the firm won a *grand prix* at the Paris exhibition of 1876 for a display that included highly praised chandeliers. About 1882 the firm began the work for which they are famous – cased or cameo glass, and had 70 glass-makers making expensive awesome pieces costing £100 or more (more than a year's wages for the average worker).

Cameo glass is made in layers, with sections of the overlaying layer cut away to reveal the layer beneath. Some pieces took many months to make, and there was a high wastage rate. Detail is sometimes

amazingly precise; the glass-makers used real flowers to copy and their figure work is superb. A number of workers were persuaded to go to America, while Bohemian immigrants formed part of the workforce. Other glass-houses in the Stourbridge area produced cameo glass. Webb cameo glass is unmistakably High Victorian, but it has a quality and a presence which probably makes it the best glass produced in Britain since the eighteenth-century drinking glass.

Much Victorian glass is anonymous, much is absurd and purposeless, but some is splendid, In the 1870s there was a reaction against extravagance and a move towards simpler more harmonious forms, as there was in ceramics. Slag glass, also known as End of Day glass was a medley of different coloured glass, or purple with grey or white veins, popularly believed to result from glass-makers using odds and ends and mixing them together and press-moulding the mix. In use from 1842, its peak of popularity was between 1875 and 1890. The important firm of Sowerby's of Newcastle-on-Tyne called their slag glass vitro-porcelain. Amberina was a shaded two-tone glass used for display as well as tableware, bronze glass was made by Webb and promoted at the 1878 Paris Exhibition, Burmese glass invented by the Mount Washington company of America was made under licence and known as Queen's Burmese because it was liked by Queen Victoria, and there were distinctive busts made in frosted glass, utterly charming.

Among the novelty glass was Candy Stripe, alternate bands of bright colour, press-moulded, cheap and sold at fairs, as was Carnival glass, usually lurid, often bright orange, and moulded with a diamond-studded finish. Little known is Clutha glass made mainly in Glasgow, produced in the 1880s and 1890s, bubbled

Above: A large transluscent green glass shallow dish and a green glass Pilgrim flask.

and streaked with a resemblance to Slag glass.

Novelties themselves included hollow glass rolling pins, originally made to hold salt with decoration on the inside. Such items were often sentimental as they frequently made gifts to girl friends and wives. Then there were the "friggers", a general name for glass-makers' novelties such as walking sticks (often hollow and filled with sweets), shoes and pipes, coaching and hunting horns, hats to hold toothpicks, pairs of swords, pieces often attributed to the glass-houses of Nailsea without much justification, and a useful novelty, the fairy light.

These were tiny lamps or table decorations, a speciality of Samuel Clarke of London from 1886 and initially made to illuminate bedrooms and nurseries at night. Egg-shaped hand coolers were fashioned in quantity, made in coloured glass as well as alabaster, marble, onyx and agate. "Witch balls" in hollow glass, found suspended in contemporary cottage doorways, are mostly fishermen's floats. Paperweights could vary from the *millefiori* type similar to those produced in France, fine-quality cameo paperweights, to cheap plain glass models with a photograph pasted on the bottom and sold in seaside resorts or at fairs. Milk glass was especially popular in America, and this white opaque glass was widely exported to the US. It was generally of a very high quality, smooth and simple. Spatter glass, pieces flecked with tiny specks of bright colour, was very much used for novelties. Vaseline glass, also known as yellow opaline, was greenish-yel-

Above: A wine glass from the second half of the eighteenth century with a round funnel bowl and an opaque twist spiral-band stem.

Opposite: A pair of green glass decanters made about 1845 when English glass was long past its best and descending into a long decline.

Left: Two Arts and Crafts Movement pieces, a bowl and a vase, by A. J. Couper and Sons, *the vase designed by the most adventurous of all nineteenth-century innovators, Christopher Dresser, involved in almost every medium, and often so advanced that his work still sometimes seems ultra-modern even by today's standards.*

Above: A display of mid-eighteenth-century colour-twist stem wine glasses. The introduction of colour into wine glasses was deplored by many of the traditionalists, though it was an inevitable path.

Opposite: Thomas Webb of Stourbridge was famous world wide for his luxury projects in glass, some of which took months to make and had a high breakage rate. He was particularly renowned for his cameo (cased) glass.

low with a glow at the edges, used for paperweights, vases and especially small bowls.

Many types of branded glass, such as Peach glass, and Primrose glass, and the blue-shaded Pearline glass were merely modish variations of already existing types. The range is immense, but a special category in Victorian glass is the scent bottle, made in pairs from the 1870s, often in cases, with one bottle containing sal volatile (smelling salts) for attacks of the vapours (fainting or imitation-fainting). Many of these, unlike novelties which were usually mould-pressed, are of the very highest quality with enamel stoppers, gold or silver mounts or filagree dressing, and of cut glass, cameo, and other pres-

tigious types. They represent Victorian glass-making at its most charming, subdued, unsensational, but immaculately made.

Victorian glass does not present a ready-made picture. It is amazingly diverse and unpredictable, and although it is traditional to sneer at the "grand machines" that grabbed the attention at international exhibitions, there is a pride in craftsmanship and attention to detail that should perhaps over-ride aesthetic prejudices. *Art nouveau* glass is a different matter, originating in the 1880s, reaching its peak about 1900, and it is so inferior to the French.

Whereas British *art nouveau* furniture can be superb, the glass is humdrum, often greenish in hue, and the critics likened it to "exploded dum-dum bullets". There is fine British *art nouveau* glass, but it tends to hide its light under a bushel and the Celtic influences which influenced metalwork and is so powerful were lacking. It was following the trend rather than making it. Fine *Art Deco* glass of the 1920s and 1930s was produced by the old-established firms such as Webb of

Above: Cut-glass basket made by Stevens and Williams of Brierley Hill in the English Black Country, a centre of glass making and including Thomas Webb a few miles away.

Stourbridge and Stuart and Sons, as well as the newcomers, and many well-known artists such as Eric Ravilous, Paul Nash, Graham Sutherland, and Laura Knight were recruited to design for them, though the most highly regarded was Keith Murray, an ex-New Zealander who brought real flair to the medium. But there was little of the panache and exuberance of American and French *Art Deco*, except in the fields of stained glass and large sand-blasted panels, such as those for the liner "*Queen Elizabeth*" designed by a little-known Birmingham artist, Dibbs. *Art Deco* glass was regarded as peripheral rather than a reflection of the prevailing ethos. In Patricia Bayer's authoritative *Art Deco Source Book* (1988) there is only one paragraph devoted to British Art Deco glass.

Good glass continues to be made in Britain, though the influences are too often Scandinavian, and so much contemporary work is schmaltzy and derivative, a debased Art Deco, and the better serious work is often in frosted glass. Although much of it has charm, and low-production glass-makers cleverly use ethnic motifs, there is no evidence that glass is today a major art form.

Opposite: Mid-Victorian cut-glass 24-light chandelier. The Victorians doted on cut glass, the sharper and more dangerous the better. In most cases it was a fad, but in a chandelier it could be very effective.

AMERICAN GLASS

Although glass was being made in Colonial America a year after the first settlers arrived from England, it was purely functional and those who made it were not necessarily experienced glass-workers but men who had only the most rudimentary instruction in the craft. Émigrés from other countries brought their own ideas, especially the Dutch who settled in New Amsterdam which later became New York, but there was no attempt to create a distinctive American style. The main products were drinking vessels, window glass and especially bottles.

Very little is known about the first American glass, but in 1739 a German immigrant, Caspar Wistar, opened a glass factory in New Jersey. Until then America had relied heavily on imports. Wistar persuaded glass-workers from Germany and Holland to join the firm. He produced mainly utilitarian ware, mostly free-blown with simple bold lines, with the favourite colours light aquamarine, green, amber and brown. A good deal of artistry was used in superimposed bands of glass in looping opaque white, blue or red glass, and a distinctive American style was being created, dependent on the English tradition, though the "lily-pad" motif (pulling the metal into a form which resembled a water-lily stem and pad) was purely American, and was adopted by many American glass-makers.

The most important American glass-maker of the time was Henry Stiegel (1729 – 1785), opening his first factory in 1763 and producing table ware, such as wine glasses, of English quality. Stiegel over-extended himself by opening a factory in 1768 in the shadows of the forthcoming war, but he had established a style not only of manufacture but of promotion, using agents in various cities and intensive advertising of a kind not seen in Britain and Europe. He died in poverty. The third important glass-maker was also of German origin,

Above: An engraved tumbler by John Frederick Amelung of the New Bremen Manufactory Maryland about 1792. The first American glass factory was opened in 1739, and Amelung was of the principal makers, opening his factory in 1784, using German and Dutch immigrant workers, though the factory closed after ten years.

Opposite: A blown and engraved tankard of the seventeenth century.

Left: Detail of the engraving from the "GMR" tumbler attributed to John Frederick Amelung, New Bremen Glass Manufactory Maryland, c. 1790–1795.

Above: A tumbler with portrait medallion set between two layers of glass by J. J. Mildner of Austria made in 1792.

Opposite: Vincenzo Lunardi made the first balloon ascent in England from Moofields, London, in 1784, and this double-walled beaker celebrating the achievement would have been made shortly afterwards, along with a host of other commemorative items such as pottery and prints.

John Frederick Amelung, who established his New Bremen Glass Manufactory near Frederick, Maryland, in 1784, unusual in that it was financed by foreign capital. The quality of his products was very high, but the factory closed after ten years, probably because of increased competition. As the nation pushed west-wards glass-houses opened; the first one beyond the Allegheny Mountains was started in 1797. Pittsburgh became an important centre of the US glass business.

Because of the increasing immigration from the conti-nent of Europe, British influences were modified by those from Germany and other countries. The first cut glass was made by Bakewell and Company of Pittsburgh in 1808, but the most influ-ential factory, which dwarfed many of its European counterparts, was the New England Glass Company. Its only real com-petitor in the US was the Boston and Sandwich Glass Company (1825 – 1889).

The most important event in American glass was the invention in 1828 by Deming Jarvis of pressed glass. This was a development of moulded glass, used as early as the first century AD, but pressed glass is forced into a mould by machine. The result is a sharp precise design and a smooth inner surface. In ordinary moulded glass the inner surface follows the mould shape. Pressed glass lent itself to mass production, where every item is identical with the next one, and a production line could be built up which could produce millions of items without retooling.

The vast array of nineteenth-century American glass owes much to the pressed glass method, and traditionally made items such as candle-sticks could be made using the new machinery, as well as uniquely American coloured flasks with embossed or inset designs such as patriotic symbols such as the eagle or historical figures, "lacy glass", again particularly American, largely used in trays and flat objects, in which the most intricate designs could be used, and the fancy glass.

Above: Although the most famous paper-weights were produced in France, the United States produced many innovatory pieces at the same period, the mid-nineteenth century when paperweights were astonishingly popular. Even the best were eventually used as door stops.

Opposite: George Washington was celebrated in every conceivable medium, including glass, and this piece, possibly an ornament without practical use, was made in Pittsburgh in 1824. As the century proceeded, glass factories moved ever westwards, and Pittsburgh was an important centre.

The fancy glass was cheap, colourful, and appealing, and was popular not only in America but throughout the world, where pressed moulding was adopted about a decade after the Americans first used it.

In lacy glass the entire background was close-stippled to make certain that any blemishes – for moulded glass can never be the equal of hand-made glass – were hidden. Moulded glass can never be mistaken for hand-made glass; the mould mark running up both sides of the piece is easy to see, and if not easy to see can be felt. The sense of touch is more reliable than eyesight, and the tiniest fault in glass or ceramics can easily be detected.

Novelty moulded glass covers a wide area, sliding into everyday ware on the one hand and emulating art glass on the other. One of the most common is Carnival glass, equally popular in Britain, so named because it was sold at fairs and similar outlets, usually in bright colours with a moulded raised-diamond design, which until recently caught the imagination of collectors who were paying large sums for fairly valueless pieces. More interesting are the multi-coloured pieces which go until a variety of names such as slag glass, agate glass, or End of Day glass. Slag glass can be ugly or it can be striking and memorable.

Another important US glass factory was Mount Washington Glass Company, established near Boston in 1837 and existing until 1958. Mount Washington was noted for its superior art glass, and was the equal of any in Britain and Europe, producing marvellous work.

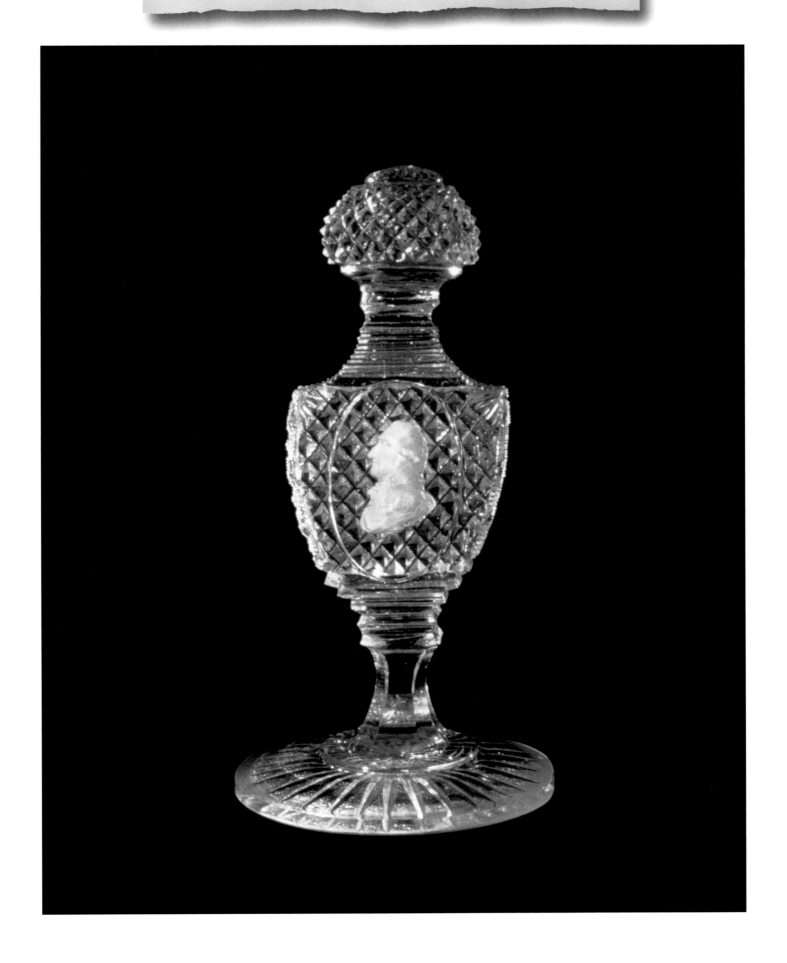

Whereas pressed glass was at the bottom of the market, imitating, sometimes innocently, hand-made glass, Mount Washington made their glass regardless of expense and using the latest technology. They created a great stir at the Philadelphia Centennial Exhibition in 1876 and were amongst the leaders in the new aesthetic period glass.

Opposite: The lily-pad motif was special to American glass, and this sugar bowl with lily-pad decoration was made probably in New York about 1830.

Amongst their best-known glass is Burmese glass, made from 1885, with a satin matt finish, and elaborate painting in coloured and gold enamel of fish and flowers. There was also a taste for Egyptian motifs. Burmese was purely a trade description and had nothing to do with Burma. Other types from other companies were Amberina (made by the New England Glass Company, and the most important "shaded" glass), Agata, Pomona, Crown Milano, and Royal Flemish, though many brand names were irrelevant and merely advertising gimmicks, sometimes minor variations on already existing glass types.

A characteristic of fine quality art glass was delicate shading, sometimes done by reheating part of the glass. Many of the rims of not only art glass but cheap novelty glass were crimped with the fingers or by using machinery before the metal solidified, and pieces were often mounted on bases of metal or other materials. Not all art glass was attractive. Some of it was vulgar and overblown, appealing to aspirations of the new rich.

One of the exponents of shaded glass was Hobbs-Brockunier of Wheeling, West Virginia, which pro-

duced some very delicate vases modelled on Chinese porcelain in the collection of Mary J. Morgan, and these are known as Peachblow. Hobbs brought shading to perfection, moving from deep red to bright yellow in barely imperceptible grades in one vase. In 1864 the firm perfected a new type of soda-lime glass which was as clear as expensive lead glass but much cheaper, and this threatened the old-established firms which continued to make lead glass. Hobbs-Brockunier also patented in 1886 an advanced mechanical crimping machine for pressed glass.

Above: The Boston and Sandwich Glass Company was one of the two most important early glass factories in the United States, noted for its enterprise as seen in this "Wheatflower" paperweight of the mid-nineteenth century.

Above: A mould-blown tie back by the New England Glass Company of Cambridge, Massachusetts, about 1855 – 1865. The New England Glass Company was, with the Boston and Sandwich Glass Company, very important in American glass history.

Left: A mould-blown flask of Bridgeton, New Jersey, from the middle years of the nineteenth century.

Opposite: The Americans invented pressed glass. It was suitable for mass production, and all kinds of unlikely objects were made cheaply and destined for a short life, such as this match safe, probably made in Pittsburgh 1876 – 1880.

Right: The Americans were adept at using glass for kitchen objects, such as this potato masher from around 1900. In Europe or Britain it would have been made of wood. or metal (if invented).

Opposite: A cut light radiator cap by J. Hoare and Company, New York, about 1887.

Overleaf: Tiffany was the great name in glass making from the late nineteenth century. Best known for its lampshades, endlessly reproduced, Tiffany was active in all the art fields of glass, including, as here, mosaic, and unlike many of the premier French makers created work on the largest of scales.

The New England Glass Company and the Boston and Sandwich Company countered the danger by introducing into their high-quality glass techniques which couldn't be imitated by pressing, such as fine engraving which would not show up in a moulded product, and brilliant cut glass with diamond-like facets, but by 1870 moulded glass looked as though it would throw traditional makers into bankruptcy.

The New England Glass Company was one of the best and largest American glass-houses, founded in 1817 by Deming Jarves and his associates. Jarves left to found the Boston and Sandwich Company in 1823. The New England firm began by making high-quality cut glass in the English style, but by the 1850s it was manufacturing display pieces which could be, and often were, taken to be Bohemian glass. In 1878 new owners took it over, and it moved to Toledo, Ohio, where the factory still survives under the name of the Libbey Glass Company.

Top-quality glass became ever more assertive and opulent, shown off at various exhibitions and trade fairs. It was soon realised by those factories involved in moulded glass that there was some glass that

Above: A plate cut in what was known as the Russian pattern by T. G. Hawkes and Company, New York 1906.

Opposite: A leaded light and bronze table lamp by Tiffany in his "Cobweb" range, one of his most characteristic pieces though his main claim to fame may lie in his masterly use of iridescent glass and organic forms.

Overleaf left: A Tiffany leaded light and bronze table lamp known as the "Zinnia" model.

Overleaf right: A water-lily paperweight by Whitall Tatus and Company of the early twentieth century.

they couldn't make. The sharpness of cut glass could not be emulated. It is not surprising that this era in glass is known as the Brilliant Period of American glass, though the taste for cut glass was universal. The various levels of the glass industry were obliged to co-exist.

Somewhat apart from art glass and novelty glass is Mary Gregory ware, allegedly named after an American glass decorator at the Boston and Sandwich Glass Company who painted enamelled figures of small children on vases, dressing-table sets, and small bowls and containers. This was widely copied throughout the world and it is difficult to ascertain the country of origin. Much of this glass was made in Bohemia, but the subjects tend to be older children while American examples show mainly infants, and are mostly of white enamel. Because of its appeal, it is widely faked. Latest research seems to indicate that "Mary Gregory" was an unknown workman at the Haln factory in Bohemia.

As in Britain there was a reaction against the high colours and complexity of the High Victorian period and a simpler glass began to be produced, sinuous, restrained, elegant, and eclectic with elements of every age and country incorporated into the pieces, however allusively. *Art nouveau* glass was refined, unpredictable, occasionally obscure, and it produced a genius, Louis Comfort Tiffany, now most noted for

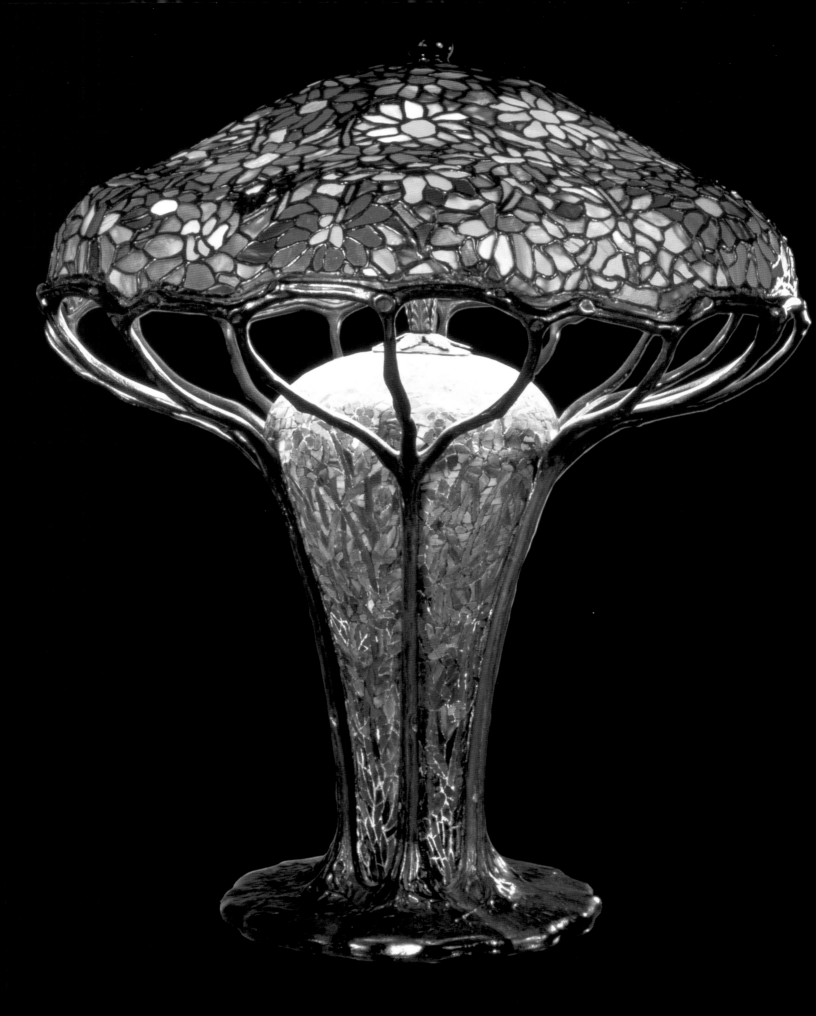

his leaded-light lamps with their mosaics of contrasting colours, still widely reproduced and never out of fashion.

Charles Louis Tiffany (1812 – 1902) was one of the great jewellers and goldsmiths of the age, by 1890 holding official appointments to 23 royal patrons, including Queen Victoria and the Shah of Persia. His son Louis Comfort (1848 – 1933) began as a painter, but inspired by William Morris's pioneer work in the Arts and Crafts Movement he turned to the decorative arts in 1878. He established a firm of interior decorators in 1879, and in a mixture of Byzantine, Moorish and Romanesque styles decorated numerous public and pri-

Above: A splendid Tiffany "Cypriot" vase of inimitable charm.

Opposite: An iridescent Tiffany paper-weight vase. The art nouveau period re-established glass as a major art form after years in the doldrums, and one of the contributions was in colour, such as the iridescent glass of Tiffany and the French makers such as Daum.

vate buildings including some rooms at the White House.

He was already working in glass, patenting an irridescent hand-made glass in 1880 which he called *favrile* (hand-made). This glass is said to have been influenced by old pharmaceutical bottles. He founded the Tiffany Furnaces in 1892. He produced stained glass on the largest of scales to designs by modern French painters such as Bonnard and Toulouse Lautrec and exhibited at Bing's Parisian shop *L'Art Nouveau* (which gave its name to the movement). He produced many vases, glass, lamps and other objects very delicately shaped and decorated with flowing abstract patterns which suggested waves,

Above: A very fetching design of 1940 by Isamu Noguchi for the prestigious US glass manufactory Steuben Glass.

Opposite: Laurence Whistler was one of the foremost English glass engravers, and this exquisite stipple-engraved goblet dates from 1963 and its style, regarded by many with scorn at the time as absurdly old fashioned.

Above: A Cod mineral-water bottle which uses a marble in the neck as a stopper (the gas in the liquid pushes the marble hard into the neck).

leaves, and feathers. He was fascinated by organic forms and the way they develop in nature. His shimmering iridescent colours were unique, and obtained by exposing the metal to the fumes of vapourised metals. He was copied in Bohemia as well as elsewhere, but Tiffany glass had a presence that was unmistakable. He was also a pioneer in glass tiles, some only an inch across, and these included "turtle-back" tiles with a slight hump. Tiffany also designed furniture, wallpaper and fabrics, and is among the most influential of designers, affecting not only *art nouveau* but *Art Deco* as well.

Somewhat surprisingly considering his great success, he devoted most of his time to jewellery after his father's death in 1902, and as in glass he occupies an important place. Whereas in Europe *art nouveau* was often spurned and the province of the forward-looking, Tiffany had a wide appeal, though his glass was made alongside traditional Brilliant Period glass, the latter being generally preferred by the mass public. American *art nouveau* glass was rarely as abstruse and form-breaking as French glass of the period, and was in general more robust *Art nouveau* glass lasted from 1895 to as late as 1925, though it lost its impetus during World War I.

Although America was less affected by the war than Europe, the changing styles and attitudes in post-war European glass had a great effect. Tiffany had influenced the rest of the world but now the new austerity and functionalism of Europe, especially the Bauhaus in Germany and Le Corbusier in France had a fall-out in the US. Much of this this functionalism was, however, countered by the gaiety and arch geometry and asymmetry of *Art Deco*. In many countries *Art Deco* was not taken seriously and regarded as a speciality of the few, a passing fad, just as *art nouveau* had been treated. However, especially in Britain and the United States there was a mass public which appreciated a commercialised version of *Art Deco* without understanding why, and although this was more important in architecture, applied graphic art such as posters, and ceramics it was also true of glass.

Perhaps the most important American *Art Deco* glass-maker was

Frederick Carder (1864 – 1963) and his Steuben Glass Works, who, like the Frenchman Lalique, encompassed both *art nouveau* and *Art Deco*. His Aurene glass dates from 1904. He introduced Cintra, Silverine, and Intarsia, and although at first Carder was strongly French influenced, he soon introduced a wholly American feel to his glass. Much of his glass contains in-built bubbles and as with French glass he utilised accidental flaws in the glass. The American glass-makers had a particular feel for geometric and streamlined pieces. The stained glass was also fine, some of it designed by the architect Frank Lloyd Wright (though he had some of it made in Holland). More than in Europe, stained glass was used in great quantities in theatres, cinemas, shop fronts, restaurants, and especially skyscrapers. Skyscrapers were regarded as the cathedrals of the twentieth century, and seemed an eminently suitable place for stained glass and massive glass panels.

The more frivolous *Art Deco* glass retains its charm, and is absurdly underrated. Functional glass has not worn well, and often seems to be more suited to a laboratory, just as functional furniture for the home looks better in an office. There were fine artists working and there were advances in glass technology. Some of the bold designs, sometimes on a massive scale using sand blasting and acid etching, are staggering, and it was on the larger public pieces rather than domestic ware that the glass industry was at its best.

"Fitness for function" has its devotees, but not a wide-ranging public. The Brilliant Period of cut glass never really ended for the wealthy and traditionally minded. After World War II influences came from Scandinavia rather than the traditional glass-making countries, and these were assimilated and manipulated, but there was not much left unknown after the 1920s and 1930s and even in domestic glass it is sometimes difficult to decide which decade a piece came from, the 1930s or the 1950s. Fine glass will always be made in all countries by dedicated designers and craftsmen, but it does not occupy the same elevated level as it once did, and it is not a process that can be carried out in a small studio as with so many art processes such as ceramics.

Above: An unusual masonic flask dating from perhaps 1815 – 1817.

EUROPEAN GLASS

By the middle of the nineteenth century Bohemia had a population of slightly more than five million. It had been over-run from time to time by the French, the Prussians, the Poles, and the Austrians. Prague was its capital and it is now part of the Czech Republic. Its glass-houses were the most important in the world.

Bohemia had succeeded Venice as the major power in glass-making, and was long celebrated for its rock crystal which it tried to emulate in glass in the Venetian style. But it was not long before Bohemian glass became distinctive, promoted by the monarchy. Its speciality was display glass and it was not much concerned with everyday utilitarian work, being imported in quantity by all the wealthy nations. Rich enamelling and engraving supplemented the intense colours of Bohemian glass, especially ruby red, and many glass-makers emigrated to neighbouring Germany, particularly Nuremberg. George I of England sent British glass-makers to Germany to acquire skills, and in turn the Germans tried to make lead glass in the manner of Ravenscroft, though they failed, unable to create the perfect proportions.

The Germans were skilled in a type of enamelling technique known as *schwarzlot* and portraits on glass in the middle of the seventeenth century were said to be as good as the finest silhouettes. In much glass of the period there was an emphasis on show. There were numerous examples of sheer bad taste, though this is what the customers wanted, especially those overseas, as they did in the nineteenth century.

Bohemian coloured glass prospered, and deep purple or black glass

Above: A Venetian enamelled dish. As soon as the glass was produced, attempts were made to copy it, not with great success.

Opposite: A Venetian enamelled dark amethyst two-handled flask from the great period, dated about 1480, and regarded with awe by the noble and the rich with good reason. Venice, a powerful country, was able to establish a monopoly in this crystal glass and rarefied colour glass, but eventually workers moved away and established glass works in other countries especially as Venice declined.

Right: A Potsdam ruby glass engraved and silver-gilt flared beaker, the glass dated about 1690, the silver-gilt mount slightly later. Central Europe, especially Germany and Bohemia, were becoming the main producers of stylish and extravagant glass for the luxury market.

Opposite: A Bohemia schwarzlot-decorated goblet of the late seventeenth century. Bohemian glass had taken on the aura of Venetian glass, and it too was copied.

called Hyalith simulated natural stone. Lithyalin had the texture, veining, and colour of marble. Bohemian glass had imitators all over the world including Britain and America, and much which passes for British or American glass (such as Mary Gregory glass) was made in Bohemia. It seemed that the Bohemian factories could manufacture and supply any kind of display glass, and there was often a desperate attempt to emulate them. This accounts for the fact that some English glass of the second half of the nineteenth century has a decidedly European feel about it.

Just as in Britain and America, the aesthetic movement of the 1870s and *art nouveau* had an impact on glass-making, though in Austria, Bohemia, and Germany it was known as the *Jugendstil*. The central European glass industry had three designers of genius, Loetz,

Above: A Dutch tazza (a shallow vessel with a foot) of the sixteenth century in the Venetian style.

Opposite: A wine glass known as a flute, with a three-quarter-length engraving of William of Orange signed, unusually, with the monogram M.

Left: A Silesian engraved goblet and cover of the period 1710 – 1715. Silesia is now mainly in Poland, but was fairly near to Bohemia, which influenced its glass houses.

Opposite: A Russian double-walled tumbler. Until the Russian Revolution and the sudden explosion of Modernism, Russian glass was not important, though the tsars employed the greatest craftsmen (such as Fabergé).

Left: Enamelled glass from Saxony or Thuringia of 1723. Enamelling on glass was a surprisingly early achievement, and was ideal for the more extravagant pieces of central Europe, and was much used in the Victorian period when added ornament on everything was a plus.

Lobmeyr of Vienna, and Moser, though often they took their lead from Tiffany of the United States. After World War I Bohemia became part of Czechoslovakia, and the glass industry prospered with the increased industrialisation for which the Czechs were famed. Czech glass was widely passed off as the work of other countries.

Some countries, prolific in other types of antiques, are surprisingly anonymous when it comes to glass, and Spain had only one major glass-house, created in 1728, and although some good crystal was produced towards the end of the eighteenth century Spanish glass is tame and unenterprising. Many Venetian glass-makers moved to the Netherlands and produced work in the Venetian style, but Holland is

Opposite: A late eighteenth-century Venetian enamelled scent flask from the Atelier of Osvaldo Brussa.

principally known for superb engraving. Their own glass was of poor quality, and there was a strong link with Britain; the British sent their fine lead glass to Holland to be engraved. High-quality display glass was made in Russia for the tsar and the nobility, but little was exported. In the aftermath of the Russian Revolution and with the encouragement of modern art, glass-makers were encouraged to produce mould-breaking progressive work, though it was a short-lived programme.

Most of the European countries could not compete with Britain and America which had developed mass production, and those countries which were industrially advanced, such as Belgium, did not make much glass. Bohemia dominated the European export market, and oddly enough this includes France. Despite their pre-eminence in the Middle Ages in stained glass, French glass before the nineteenth century is conspicuous by its absence, with little pockets in northern France of glass-houses run by Huguenots who in due course emigrated to Britain and the Low Countries. When British glass was at its peak in the eighteenth century, French glass was insipid and lack-lustre, bubbly and of low quality.

The French Revolution and the Napoleonic Wars drained France emotionally and financially and it was not until after the fall of Napoleon that major glass-houses were set up in Baccarat, St. Louis, and Clichy. Their most famous product was the paperweight, which became a great art form. In the early 1840s paperweights made in Venice were brought to France

Opposite: A Bohemian covered jar, cased, cut and gilded of the 1830 – 1840 period when glass design was beginning to lose its way.

Below: Emile Gallé was one of the greatest names in art nouveau glass. This is his "Artichaut" design.

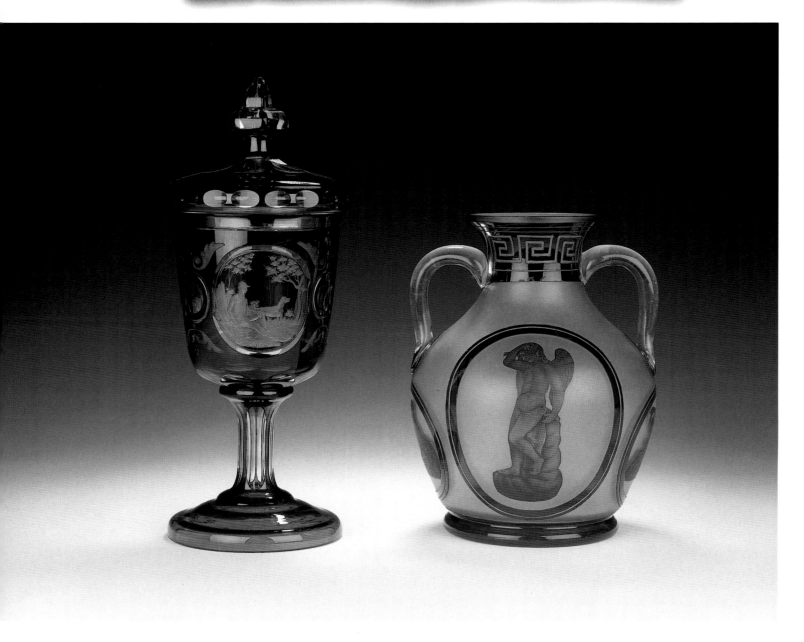

Above: Two Bohemian pieces, a vase engraved by Franz Zach, and a goblet of the second half of the nineteenth century.

Opposite: A mid-nineteenth century Bohemian stained ruby goblet engraved by August Bohm. Bohemia was especially noted for its ruby glass (also called cranberry), and it was widely copied especially in America and Britain.

and served as models, though the French surpassed the Venetians and brought incomparable ingenuity and skill to this field. In Britain and America paperweights had been amusing novelties of no great consequence. In France, probably because of the dismal record in glass, the paperweight, an article of limited use, became an icon.

Each of the factories developed their own individual styles and motifs, though the best known is *millefiori* ("thousand flowers"). Great precision is needed to set in the elements, but the effect is magnified by the apparent magic of having these flowers, insects, fruit, animals, snakes, salamanders and other motifs set inside a round or shaped transparent housing (most are round). Technically there is no comparison with the skill needed to create cameo glass.

The French exploited a niche market and these prestigious paperweights were eventually used as door stops. It was a short-lived boom – 1845-1849 – and this is part of the appeal, though Clichy went on a

Left: Viennese transparent and enamelled glass from about 1830. Austria took its inspiration mostly from the glass houses of Bohemia to the east.

little longer than the other two. The classic French paperweight did not become downgraded by the decline in taste from the 1850s. The Americans began to make their paperweights from about 1851, basing their ideas on the French models but later incorporating their own motifs.

The French designers are anonymous, though a glass-maker named Apsley Pellatt enjoyed fame for his cameos imprisoned in glass. Especially noteworthy are the "overlay" paperweights of Baccarat, in which a layer of white or coloured glass is applied to the exterior of the basic paperweight into which "windows" are cut.

These three factories also made hand-coolers and a range of display ware, but these were of no special merit. Although the French provided their quota of market-orientated display glass in the post-paperweight years there is little to mark them out. This is true of much routine nineteenth-century glass where there was a shared

Above: A Bohemian transparent and enamelled tumbler with armorial decoration of about 1835, and a Viennese topographical tumbler of a slightly earlier period.

Opposite: "Oeuvres de Lalique", a black glass plaque with moulded inscription. All Lalique pieces are signed. He combined business with fine art, and designed perfume bottles for renowned cosmetics firms such as Coty, as well as car radiator mascots, together with "pure" art such this plaque.

Above: A superb selection of Lalique pieces of great distinction.

Opposite: Spendidly decadent "Le Baiser du Faune" ("Kiss of the Faun") by Lalique for the firm of Molinard, an adventurous wheel-shape scent bottle.

European/American preference for certain styles, mostly involved in rehashing traditional forms and then mixing them up.

All this changed in France with the arrival of *art nouveau*, when seemingly out of nowhere a group of glass-makers produced a bewildering array of wholly novel pieces. The most important names are Gallé, the Daum brothers, and René Lalique. Émile Gallé studied Oriental glass at the Victoria and Albert Museum in London in 1871, visited Italy in 1877, and set up in business in 1818, producing pastiches of Venetian and Islamic glass. In 1884 he began to develop his own personal style, fantastic, visionary, emphasising the malleability of glass, and specialising in cameo glass (often grey and amethyst in colour). No two pieces were the same, and he used accidental defects

Left: Until the mid-nineteenth century French glass was undistinguished. The three glass factories of St Louis, Baccarat and Clichy suddenly sprang into prominence with their superb decorative paperweights. There had been nothing like them before though the techniques had been known since ancient times. The boom lasted only a few years.

Left: A selection of vases by Lalique: "Gros Scarabees", "Anvers" blue bowl, "Milan", "Forest" green vase, "Danaides", "Sauge", "Bacchantes", "Farandole" scent bottle.

such as bubbles and irregularities as part of the overall design. He practised every known technique except engraving, in which he was not interested. He favoured willowy flowers and plants, insects (especially dragonflies) and marine creatures such as octopuses and sea-anemones. Rarely is there a geometric shape or a straight line. Gallé also designed furniture in which, again, there is rarely a straight line, difficult as this must have been. Gallé was one of the first glass designers to sign his work, and all his work. After his death in 1904 his firm continued production, and his signature was still displayed though this time with a star. The star has often been ground away to give the impression that it is an authentic Gallé piece.

The Daum brothers produced work in the Gallé style, but not so

Above: The "Barovier Cup", a prestige blue-glass marriage cup with painted portraits of the bride and groom made when Venetian glass was at its zenith – about 1460-70.

Opposite: A carved and etched table lamp by the French maker Daum. The brothers Daum were perhaps not so adventurous as their contemporary Gallé, though this table lamp is a wonderful expression of the glass makers art. Daum continued well into the Art Deco period of the 1920s and 1930s.

117

Left: A selection of Gallé and Daum vases, showing the multiplicity of forms and the colourfulness of the designs.

Above: A Gallé cup entitled "On Such a Night as This", dated 1894. Gallé died in 1904 in his late 50s, and with him died a figure of major importance not only in glass but in applied art.

Opposite: A knobbly beaker by R. G. Ehrenfeld of Cologne about 1886, with distinct traces of a growing aversion to complexity and meaningless ornamentation.

adventurous or confident. They continued into the *Art Deco* period where they were more individualistic than in their early days. Of the three glass-makers Lalique could perhaps be the most important and certainly the most prolific, especially as he was active throughout the *Art Deco* period when he produced among other things his geometric car mascots.

Lalique established a workshop in Paris in 1885 as a jeweller, creating superb pieces right against the current fashion. To him, the settings were as important as the stones, which were often commonplace or semi-precious. He turned his attention to glass in 1902, at first scent-bottles commissioned by Coty, then vases, clocks, light fittings, statuettes, screens and panels to be set in furniture.

Right: Half a bottle of Chateau Margaux 1784, destined maybe for the wine enthusiast as there is little of note for the bottle collector.

Opposite: A highly decorated schwarzlot (enamelled) vase of indeterminate date, possibly German or Czech and post 1900.

Above: Typical of the ornate style of Venetian glass, this goblet dates from the seventeenth century. Drinking glasses in Europe often had ornate stems with protrusions, far removed from the refinement of English drinking vessels

Lalique was without prejudice, and he often worked in what was then a fairly new field, multi-media. He used the "lost wax" method of moulding, shaping pieces by hand, then melting the wax so that all pieces are one-offs and show the creative process – fingerprints, nail marks, all reproduced in the finished object. Naturally these were labour-intensive and between 1918 and 1922 Lalique built up a large glass-works at Wingen sur Modier, and although he designed the pieces he no longer created them personally. Mass-production triumphed, but they make no difference to the appeal of his opalescent nudes and sirens and his severely geometric pieces, which are often paradoxically sentimental. Lalique lived from 1860 to 1945, seeing a total transformation of taste, and able to adopt *art nouveau* for the 1920s and 1930s.

After World War I there was a constant interaction between the austere and the frivolous, "Fitness for Function" and geometry-for-fun, with sexy sensuality as an added extra, and glass was eminently suitable. There was an international style, but for the first time there was a new influence, from Sweden, with glass that was suave, smooth, and sensible, never vulgar or gaudy.

The most important glass-house in Sweden was Orresfors founded in 1898, which was at its peak between 1933-1944 under the director Viktor Lindstrand, who had studied painting under Matisse. The factory produced some of the best decorative glass in Europe bold vases with thick sides sometimes of bubbled or tinted glass with deep engraved designs. Orresfors, unlike many other prestigious factories, was willing to devote as much attention to domestic glass as display ware, and their simple facet-cut table ware of pale green and smoky brown have worn well, and provided inspiration for post-war Swedish glass.

One of the leading French glass-makers of the period was Maurice Marinot (1882 – 1960), celebrated for his thick-walled vases, jars and bottles in which, like Lalique, he used bubbles, irregularities, and chemical defects as part of the design. He also submerged his glass in acid baths to produce deep etched pieces. He worked between 1911 and 1937 and produced 2500 individual pieces; he was much copied. Gabriel Argy-Rousseau studied ceramics at Sèvres, moving into glass in 1914, making pieces of great variety though compared with Lalique some are inclined to be a little dull and a shade old-fashioned, *art nouveau* gone wrong.

An ancient Egyptian technique, *pâte-de-verre* was revived. This is powdered glass made into a paste with water and a flux, then refired in a mould, producing a crystalline effect, and many glass-makers used this method. The most characteristic *Art Deco* pieces are perhaps the chunky moulded figurines and forms, often in translucent or faintly coloured glass, but all imaginable technology was employed to please, to shock, and to serve a vague unresearched market. As in Britain and America, there was great adventure in stained glass and large sand-blasted or acid-etched panels usually for municipal buildings and prestige projects such as ocean liners.

Classic *Art Deco* glass was modified by commercial manufacturers, who thought that creating domestic and display ware in angular shapes was sufficient. This was a practice followed in furniture, ceramics, fabrics and other applied arts. As it was after World War II when any innovation, often from Orrefors in Sweden celebrated for its steely-blue thin domestic glass, was robbed of its originality and presented to as large an audience as possible. The result is bland and often pleasant, but almost everything seems to be either microwave friendly or has dim echoes of Victorian novelty ware.

Glass has produced a host of great names – Ravenscroft, Webb, Gallé, Tiffany, Lalique, Loetz – the list is almost endless – and it may be that the twenty-first century will reveal others to add to the list.

INDEX

PICTURE CREDITS